NATIONAL GEOGRAPHIC
READING EXPEDITIONS®

WILDLIFE RESCU

Ferret Rescue

By Glen Phelan
Illustrated by Tom Newsom

PICTURE CREDITS
3 (top right), 4 (top right), 5 (top right), 44 (top right), 45 (top right), 47 (top right), 48 (top right) Corbis; 3 (bottom left), 4 (bottom left), 44-45 (bottom left), 46 (bottom left), 48 (bottom left) © Creativ Studio Heinemann/ Getty Images; 3 (bottom right), 5 (bottom right), 45 (bottom right), 46 (bottom right) © Foodcollection/Getty Images; 44 Mapping Specialists, Ltd.; 45 © Jeff Vanuga/Corbis; 46 (bottom) © Mark Parchman Photography; 46 (top) © The Nature Conservancy/Associated Press; 48 © Ralph A. Clevenger/Corbis.

PUBLISHED BY THE NATIONAL GEOGRAPHIC SOCIETY
Produced through the worldwide resources of the National Geographic Society, John M. Fahey, Jr., President and Chief Executive Officer; Gilbert M. Grosvenor, Chairman of the Board.

PREPARED BY NATIONAL GEOGRAPHIC SCHOOL PUBLISHING
Sheron Long, Chief Executive Officer; Samuel Gesumaria, President; Francis Downey, Vice President and Publisher; Richard Easby, Editorial Manager; Anne M. Stone, Editor; Margaret Sidlosky, Director of Design and Illustrations; Jim Hiscott, Design Manager; Cynthia Olson, Ruth Ann Thompson, Art Directors; Matt Wascavage, Director of Publishing Services; Lisa Pergolizzi, Production Manager.

MANUFACTURING AND QUALITY CONTROL
Christopher A. Liedel, Chief Financial Officer; Phillip L. Schlosser, Vice President; Clifton M. Brown III, Director.

CONSULTANT
Mary Anne Wengel

BOOK DESIGN
Steve Curtis Design, Inc.

Published by the National Geographic Society
1145 17th Street N.W.
Washington, D.C. 20036-4688

Product #4U1005101
ISBN: 978-1-4263-5094-8

Printed in Mexico.

16 15 14 13 12
10 9 8 7 6 5 4 3 2

Contents

The Characters

Wildlife Rescue is a company that helps wild animals. They take care of animals who are sick, injured, or in danger. When the animals are ready, Wildlife Rescue returns them to the wild. This is never an easy task. Each rescue becomes an adventure. It takes our group of heroes all over the country. From the forests of the Northeast to the shores of the West Coast, Wildlife Rescue is ready to roll.

Victor Montoya is an animal expert at the County Zoo. He is also part of the Wildlife Rescue team that travels the country helping wildlife in trouble.

Susan Montoya is a veterinarian (an animal doctor). She treats injured and sick animals at the County Zoo. As a member of the Wildlife Rescue team, Dr. Montoya treats animals in the wild.

Angela Montoya is 11 years old. She hopes to be a vet like her mom. Angie likes to travel with her parents when they go on wildlife rescue missions.

Jonathan Montoya is Angie's nine year-old brother. He asks a million questions because he always wants to learn more about animals.

Jason Tenbrook works for the United States Forest Service. He is a wildlife biologist and studies how animals behave. Jason also takes care of wounded animals until they can be released back into the wild.

CHAPTER 1

On the Brink

The birthday party was in full swing. Some children were playing a bean-bag-toss game. Others were eating ice cream. Some were chasing balloons that bounced across the grass. It was a sunny June day.

Dr. Susan Montoya took a picture of the cake before cutting it. Spelled out in chocolate frosting were the words: *Happy Birthday Rocky, Randi, Duke*. Dr. Montoya looked around at everyone having a good time. The party was just about perfect. The only things missing were . . . Rocky, Randi, and Duke.

"Look! There they are!" said Angela Montoya. She pointed to a television on the wall. About 50 adults and children quickly looked up at the screen. There, lying against a pile of rags was a furry female animal about two feet long. And leaning against her side were Rocky, Randi, and Duke. It was a perfect portrait of a family of black-footed ferrets.

"They're so cute. But what are they doing?" asked one of the children.

"They are getting milk from their mother," replied Angela.

"They're so tiny," observed another.

"They sure are," agreed Victor Montoya, Angela's father. "In fact, they are no bigger than your thumb. They can't see yet either.

In another week, their white hair will become a thick tan and black fur coat. Just like their mother's. They will open their eyes a couple weeks later. Then they will see for the first time."

"Too bad. They're missing a great party," said Angela's younger brother Jonathan as he licked cake from his fingers.

Jonathan didn't see what all the fuss was about. Oh, he liked animals all right. And he loved cake and ice cream. But a birthday party for ferrets? That seemed a bit much.

Actually, the ferrets had been born four weeks earlier. The Montoyas didn't want to celebrate until they knew the young ferrets, or kits, would survive. It was important not to disturb the new family. So the Montoyas kept an eye on them with a camera in the ferret's cage. (The ferrets were really just inside the building, a few feet away.)

Dr. Montoya spoke to the crowd. "I'm sure you are all aware how important these little creatures are."

"Not me," said Jonathan as he wolfed down some more cake.

Angela nudged him, hard. "Jon!"

"Oops," he said sheepishly.

Everyone laughed.

"Well, I will explain," smiled Dr. Montoya. "Black-footed ferrets live in the Great Plains. Their numbers had been going down for years.

In 1973 the black-footed ferret was listed as an **endangered species** because there were so few left. People thought that the last wild ferret died in 1979. They thought the species was **extinct.** Just like the dinosaurs."

Then, in 1981, a rancher in Wyoming saw a small animal trying to eat from his dog's bowl. Guess what animal it was."

"A black-footed ferret!" everyone yelled.

"Right. The rancher killed the ferret. However, it proved that this animal wasn't extinct. Not yet at least."

Angela jumped up and down. "Mom, let me tell the rest," she pleaded. She loved this story.

"Go right ahead," she said with a slight bow.

"Okay. So where there's one ferret, there must be others, right? Well, people found about 130 of them living in one place. Somewhere in Wyoming. But disease wiped out almost all of them. Scientists caught the last 18 ferrets. Can you believe it? Only 18 left! It was the late

---

endangered species – an animal that may die out or become extinct
extinct – a species that no longer exists

1980s. The black-footed ferret became one of the rarest **mammals** on Earth."

"What happened to them?" asked one of her friends. She hugged a furry toy ferret. All the children had received one at the party.

"Scientists started a captive-breeding program," replied Angela.

"A what?"

---

mammal – an animal that raises its young, has a backbone, and has body hair

"A captive-breeding program. That's when scientists keep the animals safe so they can breed, or have babies. When the babies grow up, they breed with other grown-up ferrets. That way, the **population** grows."

"How many ferrets are there now?" asked one of the adults.

Angela didn't know the answer. She looked at her dad.

"About 1,000," Mr. Montoya said. "About half of them live in the wild. The rest are in zoos and conservation centers. Wildlife Rescue operates one of the conservation centers. We hope to save the black-footed ferret from extinction."

The Montoyas and their friend Jason Tenbrook run Wildlife Rescue. They help animals that are sick, injured, or in danger.

Wildlife Rescue knows their stuff. Susan Montoya is a veterinarian at a zoo in Missouri. Victor is an animal trainer at the zoo. Jason

population – a group of animals of the same species living in the same area

works as a wildlife biologist for the United States Forest Service. Angela and Jonathan help too. They feed and care for the animals as much as they can.

Jason pointed to the TV. "Raising black-footed ferrets is fairly easy. Getting them to survive in the wild is the hard part. In a few weeks, we will take the kits to a place in South Dakota. Sort of like a school."

"A school?" asked one of the youngsters. "What will they learn?"

"They will learn how to live in the wild."

CHAPTER 2

Learning to Be Wild

Every day, the ferret kits grew bigger. Their fur changed color. Soon they looked like little adults. Angela and Jonathan liked the black mask on their furry faces.

Wildlife Rescue was very careful with the ferret family. Dr. Montoya wore gloves and a facemask when she checked the kits. She didn't want to pass any germs to the ferrets.

"Can I hold them?" Angela asked her mother. It was a question she asked every day.

"Not yet. They're not strong enough."

"But they're so cute," Angela pleaded in her sweetest voice.

Her mother understood Angela's feelings. However, she did not give in. "Angela, these animals are very special and not just because they're cute. If they get hurt or sick, they won't stand a chance in the wild."

"I know, I know," said Angela.

The young ferrets were now six weeks old. They had opened their eyes and could see. They were now allowed to spend time outdoors. Angela laughed as she watched the ferrets run around in their fenced-in pen.

The ferrets were so funny when they played. They chased one another around and around. Sometimes they would try to sneak up on each other from behind. A kit would slowly creep toward its brother or sister. Then with a burst of energy, the kit would throw itself forward. Sometimes the "attacker" would miss and land in a ball of fur and dust. Angela couldn't help but giggle.

Dr. Montoya enjoyed the young ferrets' antics too. She was glad to see them play for another reason though. "Do you see what they're doing?" she asked Angela.

"Yeah. Playing."

"Right." Her mother smiled. "But they are also learning skills. See how they sneak up on each other? They are learning how to hunt. When they run from each other, they are learning how to escape **predators.** They're going to need those skills in the wild."

The kits mostly slept during the day. By early evening, though, they were up and ready

predators – animals that hunt and eat other animals

to go. Angela and Jonathan watched them every evening. It was much better than TV.

Rocky was Jonathan's favorite kit. He was the fastest and strongest. Jonathan cheered every time Rocky caught his brother or sister.

Angela's favorite was Randi. She was darker than her brothers. And her mask wasn't quite even. Angela thought she was the cutest. She felt sorry for her though. Randi wasn't as fast as her brothers. She would always get caught.

Angela worried that she might not do well in the wild. She mentioned it to her parents one evening at dinner.

"I wouldn't worry about it," her dad said. "It's too early to tell how any of the kits will do on their own. We'll get a better idea when we see how they act at the conservation center in South Dakota. Are you kids all packed?"

"Are you kidding? We've been packed for three days!" Angela exclaimed.

They left early the next morning. Everyone was excited about the trip. Victor and Susan Montoya rode in the front seat of the Wildlife Rescue truck. Angela and Jonathan rode in the back along with Jason and three special furry friends.

By early afternoon, they were riding through the prairie lands of Nebraska. At least, that's what they used to be. Farm fields had long replaced most of the prairie grasses.

Angela noticed Jason looking quietly out the window. She wondered what he was thinking about. Jason was a Native American. His ancestors used to live on these plains. Maybe he was imagining a herd of bison roaming through tall prairie grass.

Jonathan broke the silence. "Look at all the cattle." Dozens of brown-and-white cattle grazed in a nearby pasture.

"Yep. This part of the Great Plains is almost all farms and ranches now," said Mr. Montoya.

"That's why the black-footed ferrets are endangered, right?" asked Angela.

"Yes, that's a big reason," agreed Dr. Montoya. "The farms and ranches replaced the ferrets' natural **habitat**. So there are fewer places for them to live."

Jason spoke up. "But that's only part of the story." He looked at the young ferrets sleeping in the carrying case. "Black-footed ferrets need more than a place to live. They depend on other animals called prairie dogs. Do you remember what prairie dogs look like?"

"Sure," said Jonathan. "We see them at the zoo all the time. They look like big chipmunks or squirrels. What do they have to do with ferrets?"

"Prairie dogs are the main food for black-footed ferrets," replied Jason.

"Really?" Angela was surprised.

---

habitat – a place where a plant or animal naturally lives and grows

"Yes. Prairie dogs dig holes in the ground, called burrows. That's where they live. At night, black-footed ferrets hunt the prairie dogs in their burrows. The ferrets live in the burrows that don't have prairie dogs."

Jonathan shrugged his shoulders. "Okay, so what's the problem?"

"The problem is that there aren't as many prairie dogs as there used to be," their dad said.

"Because of all the farms and ranches?"

"Yes. But also because many ranchers consider prairie dogs to be pests. They eat some of the grass that cattle would eat. So some ranchers try to get rid of the prairie dogs. They shoot them or poison them."

"Gross!" cried Angela.

"Do you think we'll see any prairie dogs?" asked Jonathan.

"I'm sure of it. The place we're going is right next to a prairie dog town."

CHAPTER 3

A Wild Night

The sun was going down as Wildlife Rescue pulled up to the conservation center. A woman dressed in jeans, a jacket, and boots came out to meet them.

"Hi everyone. I'm Rita Rossi, the director of this conservation center. Welcome to South Dakota, we've been expecting you." After friendly greetings, Rita took everyone on a tour.

"The most important parts of our center are the pens where the ferrets learn how to live in the wild." Rita pointed to several large pens. Each one was about the size of a school gym. Angela and Jonathan ran up to one of them. Through the fencing they could see many holes dug into the ground. A small mound of soil surrounded each hole.

"Are those burrows?" Angela asked.

"Yes, they are," replied Rita. "The burrows are the entrances to underground tunnels. Prairie dogs dig them. Each pen is a small prairie dog town. Of course, it's not like a town with buildings and streets. It's an area where prairie dogs live together."

"Look! There's one!" Jonathan pointed through the fence. A prairie dog had popped its

head out of its burrow to look around. Then it ducked back down. A couple more nibbled at the grass near a burrow.

"So what do they do in the pens?" asked Angela.

"This is where the black-footed ferrets learn how to hunt. In the wild, the mother teaches them. But coyotes, hawks, and other predators might kill the ferrets. Here in the pens, the kits are protected."

"Where are the ferrets?" Jonathan was straining his eyes to see in the dimming light.

"They're just waking up about now. During the night, they move from burrow to burrow looking for sleeping prairie dogs."

Jonathan noticed a group of people loading some equipment into a van. "What's that?" he asked, pointing to the van.

"We're taking a ferret survey tonight. There's a large prairie dog town a couple miles from here. It's one of the places where we release our ferrets into the wild. A few times a year we go out there and see how many ferrets we can find. Then we can tell if the ferret population is growing. The survey teams are loading powerful spotlights. The ferrets' eyes glow green in the light."

"Cool!" Jonathan was impressed.

Rita had an idea. "Hey, how would you like to join us tonight? Most of the survey teams are volunteers. We can always use more counters."

Jonathan and Angela turned toward their parents. "Can we? Please?"

"I don't know. It can be dangerous out there at night," said Dr. Montoya.

Jason came to the rescue. "I'll go with them. We'll be a team."

That was fine with the Montoyas.

"Terrific," said Rita. "Come on. I'll introduce you to some of the others."

An hour later, Jason, Angela, and Jonathan stood on the edge of a prairie dog town. The sky was black, but spotlights lit up large areas of the ground. Bushes cast deep, dark shadows. Was anything hiding in there? It was hard to tell.

"It's kind of spooky," whispered Angela.

Jonathan thought so too, although he didn't admit it.

Suddenly an animal popped its head up out of a burrow. It was 100 feet away. It was hard to tell exactly what animal it was. The green glow from its eyes, however, left no doubt.

"A ferret!" Jonathan yelled.

"Jon, quiet," said Angela in a loud whisper.

The ferret looked right at them. Then it quickly looked away. Something caught its attention. Jason noticed a bush rustling ten feet from the burrow.

All of a sudden an animal jumped from the bush toward the ferret. Jason saw that it was a bobcat. Another leap and the bobcat was only inches away. Quick as a flash, the ferret ducked back down its burrow. The bobcat's claws grabbed nothing but dirt.

The bobcat sniffed at the hole for a few seconds. Then it went to three or four other burrows. “It’s seeing if the ferret is going to pop up someplace else,” Jason said quietly. “But the ferret is smart enough to stay underground where the bobcat can not go.”

After a couple minutes, the bobcat gave up. It walked out of view and into the darkness. This was just the beginning of a wild night.

Angela and Jonathan now looked closely at every bush, at every burrow. Suddenly a sound came from right behind them. . . . *PHLUUM!*

Angela jumped. A large bird swooped down past her left shoulder. It was so close she could feel the breeze.

“Owl,” said Jason.

The owl touched down twenty feet in front of them. Its legs were stretched out. Then the owl flew up and away with a mouse in its claws.

“You okay, Angie?” Jason asked.

“I . . . I think so. That owl just surprised me, that’s all.”

“Wow! How did the owl even see that mouse?” Jonathan asked. “I can’t see much, even with the lights.”

"Owls have good eyesight," replied Jason. "They are adapted to seeing at night, just like the ferrets."

Angela and Jonathan wished they had owl eyes. Now they were on the lookout for anything that walked, jumped, flew, or crawled in the night. Their eyes darted this way and that way.

"Relax, kids. You're going to get dizzy. Besides, you'll miss the ferrets." Jason chuckled quietly. He could tell they were nervous.

They watched another 10 minutes in silence. Then Jason turned his head slightly. "What is it, Uncle Jason?" Angela whispered. He put his finger to his lips. "Shhh. Listen."

Then they heard it, a weak barking sound. Jason scanned the area with his binoculars. "There." He pointed and handed the binoculars to Angela. At the edge of the lighted area, she could see another black-footed ferret. It was barking at a fox. Then the ferret turned and raised its tail. The fox quickly trotted away.

"I didn't know ferrets bark," said Angela.

"Sure. They bark or hiss to scare away an attacker. If that doesn't work, they turn around and spray a smelly chemical. Not as bad as a skunk, but it works."

Some of the volunteers were staying out all night. Not Jason and the kids. They were tired from their long trip. They went back to the conservation center at midnight. Angela and Jonathan had a lot to tell their parents in the morning.

CHAPTER 4

Escape!

Jonathan hopped down from the top bunk. He tried to be quiet. The volunteers who had stayed out all night were asleep.

"Angie, wake up," Jonathan nudged his sister on the bottom bunk. She was groggy at first, but soon shook off her sleep. They were looking forward to a fun day. They had no idea how exciting it was going to be.

Angela and Jonathan met their parents and Jason for breakfast in the small cafeteria. They told them all about the night before.

"No kidding. The owl almost knocked me over!" Angela swiped her hand past her ear to show how close their feathered friend had come. "I never heard it until it flew by."

"That's the first time I've seen an owl in the wild," Jonathan exclaimed.

"Or a bobcat," said Angela. "It was so cool."

Jason decided not to remind the children how nervous they had been. It's good to be a little nervous about the wilderness, he thought. It keeps you on your toes. It reminds you to respect wild animals.

"Kids, you're leaving out the best part," Jason said. "We saw two black-footed ferrets, remember? Rita says that makes twelve so far this week. That's three more than last fall. So the number of ferrets is growing."

"I never knew there were so many predators looking for ferrets," said Angela.

"Yes, and we saw only a few of them," said Jason. "Ferrets have to be on the lookout for lots of animals. Like coyotes, foxes, badgers, hawks, snakes, . . ."

"Whoa, I get it, I get it," said Jonathan.

"Will Randi and her brothers learn how to escape from all of those animals?" Angela looked worried.

"Oh, I think so, with the right training," said her mother. "In fact, Rita said you can help with

the training today. Finish breakfast and we'll go over to the pen."

Training turned out to be more like playing. It included chasing the ferret kits with a stuffed badger. The badger was tied onto a remote-controlled toy car. The scary-looking badger made the kits run away. Angela and Jonathan took turns controlling the "robo-badger," as Rita called it.

Jonathan was better at it than Angela. He played a lot with a remote-controlled car at home. He was an expert.

"Don't run the badger all the time," said Rita. "You don't want to get the kits too tired. Move slowly at first, like you're sneaking up on them. Then move suddenly."

"I get it," said Angela. "Just like a real badger would do."

"Exactly."

The idea was to train the kits to duck into a burrow to escape danger. Rocky and Duke didn't catch on too quickly. They preferred to run around and jump *over* the burrows. Randi learned quickly though. After being chased a couple times, she always ran into the nearest burrow and stayed hidden.

They trained with the robo-badger for 20 minutes. Rita said they could have another session in the evening. However, those plans ended up changing. . . .

"They're gone!" Angela came running into the office where her mom, dad, and Jason were talking with another scientist. "They're gone!" she repeated.

"Who's gone?" asked her mom.

"Rocky, Randi, and Duke! Jon and I went to check on them and the gate was open. They're gone! Come see!"

They all ran back to the pen. The gate was open like Angela had said. Rita came running up. She was carrying some sort of box with a cable coiled around it.

"I just heard about it. The kits probably escaped, but we have to make sure. Victor and Susan, can you use this camera to check all the burrows and tunnels? Jason, Angela, and Jonathan, you can start looking around in this area for the kits. I'm going to round up some volunteers to help with a bigger search."

Rita shook her head. "Someone must have forgot to close the gate after feeding the kits. That was an hour ago. Okay, let's move."

Victor and Susan went from burrow to burrow in the pen. They pushed the cable into each burrow. The cable had a tiny video camera at its tip. The box was a video screen. They found two sleepy prairie dogs in the tunnels, but no ferrets.

Meanwhile, Jason, Angela, and Jonathan searched the ground just outside the pen. Jason found ferret tracks in the sandy soil near the open gate. He showed Angela and Jonathan what they looked like.

"Okay. Let's spread out. Walk slowly so that you don't cover up the tracks. If you see tracks going off in one direction, call me over."

It was tough following the tracks, even for Jason. A bunch of tracks went off in one direction, but then doubled back. Some tracks criss-crossed. Finally, they found tracks that continued in one direction. Away from the pen, though, the ground became harder and grassy. There were no tracks to be found.

Then, a stroke of luck.

"Hey, over here!" called Jonathan. He came upon a sandy patch. There were tracks in it. Several bushes lay a few feet from the patch. The branches of one of the bushes started moving. Jonathan peeked around it. There, tugging at the branch, was Duke.

Jonathan bent over to pick him up as Jason and Angela came over. "Don't touch him, Jon. I'll get him." Jason put on a pair of leather gloves he had in his back pocket. Then he carefully and expertly picked up the playful little animal.

"Good work, Jon," he said with a smile.

"Yeah, Jon, way to go." Angela gave him a friendly tap on the arm.

Jason placed Duke back in the pen and closed the gate. Victor and Susan had just finished their search with the camera.

"One down, two to go," said Susan.

Just then, Rita came running up with about a dozen volunteers. Everyone had flashlights, gloves, and cell phones. Rita took charge.

"Okay. I need two people to stay near the pen in case the kits come back. We'll set up all the spotlights here and shine them out into the prairie as far as possible. Break up into pairs. Keep your eyes and ears open. Let's go."

It was almost 8 o'clock and getting dark. Angela and Jonathan searched with their mom. Everyone knew that Rocky and Randi would likely be killed if they weren't found soon. It was a race against time.

CHAPTER 5

A Chance to Be Free

A half hour later, Dr. Montoya's cell phone rang. "Hello? . . . Really? . . . Great, I'll be sure to tell them. Bye."

She closed her phone. "Someone has found Rocky. He seems to be in good shape. Now we're only looking for Randi."

It was dark now. The spotlights were way behind them, like distant streetlights. Flashlights lit the way.

Angela slowly swept her light in front her. "Huh," she gasped. There, standing on a rock, was a large hawk. It turned its head toward the light. Then it let out a loud squawk and flew away. It reminded Angela of all the predators that were out tonight, looking for a meal.

Angela pointed her flashlight at the rock as they passed. For the second time, she gasped. Two beady, green eyes stared out at her from beneath the rock. Looking more closely, she could see the crooked mask of Randi.

"Mom, Jon, look!" Angela was overjoyed. Dr. Montoya carefully coaxed Randi out of her hiding place. She then picked her up. "She must have ducked under the rock to get away from the hawk," Dr. Montoya said.

"I knew she was smart," said Angela proudly. "She can teach her brothers a thing or two."

Back at the center, everyone was relieved. It had been a long evening, but no one was tired. It was time to celebrate.

"I have some fudge ripple ice cream for just such an occasion," announced Rita. That was the perfect ending to the evening.

Over the next few days Angela and Jonathan helped train the kits. They had a great time

helping to care for the other ferrets too. However, soon it was time to go home.

Six ferrets were being released the day Wildlife Rescue was leaving. These ferrets had been at the center for nine months. They had learned how to hunt prairie dogs. They knew how to avoid predators. Still, many black-footed ferrets don't survive more than a few weeks after being released. Everyone was concerned, but hopeful.

Rita and Dr. Montoya placed a radio transmitter around the neck of each ferret. Jonathan thought it looked like a wristwatch. "What's that for?" he asked.

Rita explained. "This transmitter gives off signals. The signals show up as bleeps on a monitor. That way, we can track where the ferrets go."

"And tell if they survive," added Dr. Montoya.

"Well, good luck little ferret buddies," said Jonathan.

On the way to the truck, Wildlife Rescue stopped to say goodbye to Rocky, Randi, and Duke. Their time to be released was still months away. In the meantime, they would continue to learn to be wild.

Wildlife Rescue had been home for a few days when they got a call from Rita. "So far, so good," she said in a bright voice. "The bleeps on the monitor show that the ferrets are moving around. They go from burrow to burrow in search of prairie dogs. Just like they should.

Hopefully, the ferrets will have kits next spring. Then the mothers will do what mother black-footed ferrets should do. They will teach their kits to be wild."

The Facts Behind the Story

Black-footed Ferrets

At one time black-footed ferrets lived on the prairies and grasslands throughout the Great Plains of the United States. Now they are one of the rarest mammals in the world. People changed this animal's habitat when they moved into the prairies and used the land for farming. The prairie dogs and their tunnels were a nuisance for farmers, so they worked to get rid of them. This left the black-footed ferrets with fewer places to live and fewer prairie dogs to eat.

Ferrets Head to Tail

The black-footed ferret has soft, yellow-brown fur with black on its feet and the tip of its tail. Around its eyes is a black mask. It has a slim body and long tail. It grows to be about two feet long. Black-footed ferrets move very quickly and have keen senses of hearing and smell. Their senses help them hunt underground and find prey in the dark.

What Ferrets Eat

Sometimes black-footed ferrets eat mice or rabbits, but prairie dogs are the ferret's main food. Prairie dogs live in large groups in underground burrows connected by many tunnels. During the day, black-footed ferrets curl up in empty prairie dog burrows. At night, the ferrets quietly slip through the tunnels and catch prairie dogs. One black-footed ferret can eat about 100 prairie dogs in a year.

Baby Ferrets

Baby ferrets are called kits. A mother black-footed ferret has a litter of three or four kits at the beginning of summer. She nurses them in a burrow until they are ready to eat meat. In fall when the kits are fully grown they leave their mother. They now live on their own.

Read, Research, and Write

Write A Class Report

Think about what you have learned about black-footed ferrets. Imagine that you are making a one-minute class report about these endangered animals. What information would you include in your report?

Copy the web below. In each circle, write a fact about black-footed ferrets. Use the web to write a script for your class report.

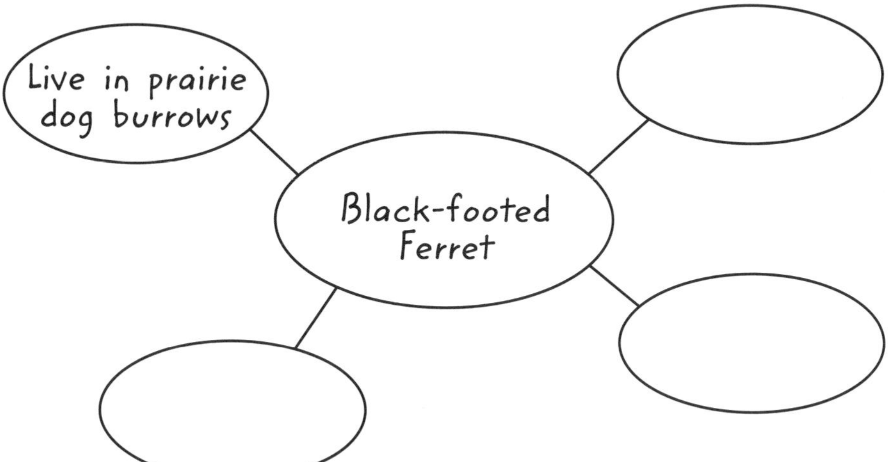

Extend Your Reading

Read More About Black-footed Ferrets

Find and read more books about black-footed ferrets. As you read, think about these questions. They will help you understand more about this topic.

- How are black-footed ferrets alike and different from other North American predators?
- How does a mother black-footed ferret feed her kits?
- Where do black-footed ferrets find their mates?
- What other mammals live underground?

SUGGESTED READING
Reading Expeditions
Life Science: Life Cycles